MW01710209

Rapture

Joe Crews

ONE
WHY WOULD JESUS PROMISE?

There is a theological question that has disturbed millions of Christians and has lent untold doctrinal confusion to the modern religious world. That question revolves around the manner of Christ's coming back to this earth at the end of the world. Multitudes have been led to believe that Christ will return secretly. What about the so-called secret rapture? A large number of Christians have been exposed to this "dispensationalist" or "futurist" interpretation of prophecy and have been hopelessly confused.

According to this view, the coming of Jesus will be in two separate events. First, He will come secretly to take the church to heaven, and then, seven years later, He will come in an open demonstration of power and glory. In between those two events, the Antichrist is supposed to come into power and the great tribulation period takes place.

But the truth is that the Bible nowhere speaks of these two separate comings of

Jesus. There is no second stage of His coming that occurs seven years after the so-called "rapture." By the way, that word "rapture" is also an invention of theologians. It can't be found in the Bible in even a single instance. It is a word coined for the second advent of Jesus.

Now here is what we find in the Scriptures: Christ's coming, the resurrection, and catching up of the saints to meet Jesus in the air, all take place at the same time, at the end of the world. This is why Jesus said, "Lo, I am with you alway, even unto the end of the world" (Matthew 28:20). Now why would Jesus promise to be with the church until the end of the world if He intended to come seven years before the end to take them out of the world? The promise would have no meaning.

TWO
WILL IT BE SECRET?

The secret rapture doctrine contradicts the words of Christ in Matthew chapter 13 when He said that the wheat and tares would grow together until the "end of the world" and then would be separated. According to the two-stage teaching of His coming, both groups would *not* grow together until the end of the world. The righteous would be separated from the wicked seven years before the end. And what about the promise of the resurrection? Christ said, concerning the righteous, "And I will raise him up at the last day" (John 6:40). No one denies that this means the last day of the world. Yet Paul declares that the saints are caught up to meet the Lord at the same time the dead in Christ are raised. He says, "For the Lord himself shall descend from heaven with a shout, with the voice of the archangel, and with the trump of God: and the dead in Christ shall rise first: Then we which are alive and remain shall be caught up together with them in the clouds to meet the Lord in the air" (1 Thessalonians 4:16, 17).

Please keep in mind that Jesus called this resurrection the "last day." But how could it be the "last day" if this gathering of the saints takes place seven years before the end of the world? And how could the "last trump" sound if it really wasn't the very last moment of time?

Can you imagine the graves opening and the righteous rising and no one knowing that it had occurred? And consider this additional testimony of the Word of God:

- **Revelation 6:16, 17** When the wicked see Christ come, they cry out to the rocks and mountains, "Fall on us, and hide us from the face of him that sitteth on the throne, and from the wrath of the Lamb: For the great day of his wrath is come; and who shall be able to stand?"
- **Matthew 24:27** "For as the *lightning* cometh out of the east, and *shineth* even unto the west; so shall also the coming of the Son of man be."
- **1 Corinthians 15:52** "For the *trumpet* shall *sound*, and the dead shall be raised."
- **Psalm 50:3** "Our God shall come, and shall *not keep silence*."

- **Revelation 1:7** "Every eye shall *see* him."
- **Matthew 24:30** "Then shall all the tribes of the earth *mourn,* and they shall *see* the Son of man coming in the clouds of heaven with power and great glory."
- **Matthew 24:31** "He shall send his angels with a great *sound of a trumpet,* and they shall gather together his elect from the four winds, from one end of heaven to the other." (This is clearly the time when Christ comes to gather His saints.)

To say that the second coming of Christ to gather His saints will be secret, in view of these clear texts of Scripture, and in the absence of any text that even hints at His coming being secret, is to deny the Bible as the Word of God. In an attempt to uphold their contrived theory, the rapturists quote Matthew 24:40, 41 out of context. Notice this entire passage:

"But as the days of Noe were, so shall also the coming of the Son of man

> be. For as in the days that were before the flood they were eating and drinking, marrying and giving in marriage, until the day that Noe entered into the ark, And knew not until the flood came, and took them all away; so shall also the coming of the Son of man be. Then shall two be in the field; the one shall be taken, and the other left. Two women shall be grinding at the mill; the one shall be taken, and the other left" (Matthew 24:37–41).

Jesus is clearly drawing a parallel between the second coming and the days of Noah. Those who entered the ark in Noah's day were saved, and those who refused to enter the ark were left outside. But what were they left for? For another chance? No, obviously they were left to be destroyed by the Flood. So, says Jesus, will it be when He comes at the end of the world. One will be taken to heaven with Jesus, and the other will be left for destruction. Verse 51 makes clear what will happen to those who are left: "And shall cut him asunder, and appoint him his portion with the hypocrites: there shall be weeping and gnashing of teeth." Read Luke 17:26–37 for Luke's parallel account of these same words of Jesus. In verse 36, this statement is made: "Two men shall be in the field; the one shall be taken, and the other left." Now notice verse 37 and the question the disciples asked: "And they answered and said unto him, Where, Lord?" They wanted to know where those who didn't go to heaven were going to be left. Notice Jesus' clear answer: "And he said unto them, Wheresoever the body is, thither will the eagles be gathered together."

Take note how Jesus taught that the bodies of the wicked are going to be left on the ground for the eagles to consume. Scripture is too plain to be misunderstood. Only as we accept all that the Bible says can we be safe from such deceptive teachings that are confusing millions of sincere Christians today concerning this most glorious event of all ages, the second coming of Jesus Christ.

Now, I realize that the rapturists hang onto the texts that liken the Lord's coming to "a thief in the night." They assume that this must be a quiet, secret coming. But does it really mean that? Let's show that it definitely does not. Here is one of those texts in 2 Peter 3:10: "The day of the Lord will come as a thief in the night; in the which the heavens shall pass away with a great noise, and the elements shall melt with fervent heat." Obviously the "thief" part has nothing to do with secrecy because the heavens will pass away with a great noise! And if coming "as a thief" is the secret rapture which takes place seven years before the end of the world, how can the heavens and earth "pass away," as Peter describes it? The heavens and earth could not pass away seven years before the world ends—that is the end!

The fact is that Jesus Himself explained clearly just how a thief's coming could be related to His coming: "Watch therefore: for ye know not what hour your Lord doth come. But know this, that if the goodman of the house had known in what watch the thief would come, he would have watched, and would not have suffered his house to be broken up" (Matthew 24:42, 43). There it is, so plain and simple! The thief would come unexpectedly when the owners were not looking for a thief. In the same way, His coming would take people by surprise. They would not be watching or looking for it.

THREE
WILL CHRIST RETURN IN TWO PHASES?

The dispensationalists teach that the two separate stages of Christ's coming are indicated "in the Greek." They argue that there will first be the rapture (parousia), a secret coming; then seven years later will be the revelation (apokalupsis), His coming in power and glory. But, actually, instead of teaching two separate events, the Greek terms are used interchangeably in the Bible. They give no indication of a seven-year interval.

For example, Paul uses the word "parousia" in the famous rapture chapter of 1 Thessalonians 4 in speaking of the coming of our Lord and our gathering together unto Him. He then goes right on to show that this "parousia" will destroy the man of sin. Speaking of the Antichrist, Paul says, "whom the Lord shall … destroy with the brightness of his coming [parousia]" (2 Thessalonians 2:8). These texts clearly describe the coming (parousia) of Christ as taking place after the reign of the man of sin, not as an escape rapture before the reign of the Antichrist begins.

The other Greek word "apokalupsis" (revelation) is used in a way that indicates it is not a separate coming from the time the believers are gathered up. Peter said to "be sober, and hope to the end for the grace that is to be brought unto you at the revelation [apokalupsis] of Jesus Christ" (1 Peter 1:13). Why would Christians be exhorted to keep hoping to the very end of the world for the grace brought through the *revelation* of Christ if their real hope was a secret rapture seven years before the *revelation?*

Now look at some verses that prove beyond a doubt that the two words "parousia" and "apokalupsis" refer to the same event. In Matthew 24:37 we read, "But as the days of Noe were, so shall also the coming [parousia] of the Son of man be." Luke's account of the same passage says, "As it was in the days of Noe … Even thus shall it be in the day when the Son of man is revealed [apokalupsis]" (Luke 17:26, 30). This shows that the coming (parousia) of Christ and the revelation (apokalupsis) of Christ are the same event. There is absolutely no basis for placing seven years in between.

Many dispensationalist teachers actually claim that the rapture is not really the "coming" of Jesus at all. They say His coming is when Christ returns in power seven years after the rapture. But what a contradictory, confusing explanation that is! The fact is that there are many Scriptures that admonish Christians to wait and watch for the coming of the Lord. For example, James 5:7 says, "Be patient therefore, brethren, unto the coming of the Lord." But why should Christians need to be patient unto the coming of the Lord if there is to be a secret rapture to take them to heaven seven years before His coming?

Strange as it may seem, this whole counterfeit secret rapture is built upon a constant repetition of words and ideas that are not found in the Bible at all. But they have been repeated so often that millions have assumed that they must be soundly biblical. Let's take a look at some of the texts that have been used to support the doctrine of a two-phase coming of Christ. And please notice that none of the verses actually say what some try to read into them. In fact, it is only after a person has already assumed that Christ will return in two separate comings that these verses could even suggest the idea.

Revelation 3:10 is often quoted to try to prove that the righteous will be taken out of the world before the tribulation. "Because thou hast kept the word of my patience, I also will keep thee from the hour of temptation, which shall come upon all the world, to try them that dwell upon the earth." It is immediately obvious that this text does not speak of the righteous leaving this world at all. Jesus completely clarified the meaning by something He said in John 17:6, 15 which sounds very similar. "They have kept thy word … I pray not that thou shouldest take them out of the world, but that thou shouldest keep them from the evil." Don't miss the significance of the term "kept the word" in both these texts. Both statements are talking about the same group of people—the faithful ones.

Now if those who "kept the word" can be "kept from the evil" of the world without being taken out of the world, why should we suppose that a special coming and secret rapture is required for those who "kept the word" to be "kept from the hour of temptation"? Whatever else may be taught in Revelation 3:10, it is evident that no extra coming of Christ is indicated.

True biblical doctrine must be based upon clear statements of what the entire Bible teaches on a subject and not upon verses that offer only veiled inferences. Luke 21:36 is an example of that very thing. Jesus said to His disciples, "Pray always, that ye may be accounted worthy to escape all these things that shall come to pass." How? By a secret rapture to take them to heaven seven years before the end of the world? Definitely not, for in the prayer of

Jesus we read, "I pray not that thou shouldest take them out of the world, but that thou shouldest keep them from the evil." When He told them to "pray … to escape," He must have meant the same as when He prayed, "I pray not … take them out of the world but … keep them." This rules out a secret rapture entirely. The text that is used to prove the rapture is seen actually to forbid the saints being taken out of this world during the time of trouble.

FOUR
THE SEVEN-YEAR TRIBULATION

Since so much rapturist theology revolves around the seven-year period, one would assume that the Bible must speak frequently of such a time period. But not so. There is not one single scriptural reference that ties the seven years to the end of the world or the coming of Christ. Most rapturist literature mentions the seven-year tribulation period without offering any Bible proof or explanation. Millions have assumed that it must be so well documented that no proof is needed. In fact, the opposite is true. There just isn't any evidence to give.

Most Bible students are amazed to learn that the rapturists try to justify their seven years by lifting a prophecy of Daniel completely out of its context. In Daniel 9:24–27 God made a daring prophecy concerning the probation of the nation of Israel. He said to Daniel, "Seventy weeks ['weeks of years' RSV] are determined upon thy people … to finish the transgression, and to make an end of sins" (v. 24). Please notice that God was going to allow Daniel's people seventy weeks to see what they would do with the Messiah when He appeared. The seventy weeks are prophetic time, and each day represents a literal year (Ezekiel 4:6). So the seventy weeks would be a literal period of 490 years, after which the Israelites would no longer be God's people. They would be rejected as a nation because of their rejection of the Messiah.

Don't miss the point in Daniel 9:25 that the prophecy of the seventy weeks was to begin with the decree to restore and build Jerusalem. That well-known date is 457 B.C., when Artaxerxes sent out the decree (Ezra 7:13). From that date, 457 B.C., the Jews would have exactly 490 years to finish filling up their cup of iniquity by rejecting the Messiah. That 490-year probation ended in A.D. 34, and the Jews ceased to be God's chosen people. Daniel 9:25 says that the Messiah would be anointed after sixty-nine of those prophetic weeks had passed by. That would be 483 years from the decree date of 457 B.C. It takes no mathematician to figure the end of that prediction. It brings us to the year A.D. 27, the very year that Jesus was baptized by John and the Holy Spirit anointed Him for His ministry. Since "Messiah" means "Anointed One," this had to be the fulfillment of Daniel's prophecy that the Messiah would appear in A.D. 27.

Now mark this fact: seventy weeks were assigned to the Jewish probation, but Christ appeared as the Messiah after sixty-nine weeks. That leaves the seventieth week for Christ to minister *before the Jews' probation ended.* What was to happen in the seventieth week? Daniel 9:27 tells us, "And he shall confirm the covenant with many for one week: and in the midst of the week he shall cause the sacrifice and the oblation to cease."

The midst of the week would be three and a half prophetic days (literal years) from His baptism. And according to the Bible, the ministry of Jesus lasted for three and a half years. In the spring of A.D. 31 He was crucified. The veil of the temple was rent (Matthew 27:51), signifying the end of sacrifices. By His death He caused them to cease. Another three and a half years would lead up to the end of the seventy weeks and the end of Jewish probation. During that three and a half years the disciples labored largely for the Jews. But in A.D. 34 the seventy weeks ended; Stephen was stoned and the gospel began to go to the Gentiles (Acts 8:4). The Jews had rejected the gospel message and were no longer God's people—just as Daniel had predicted. Henceforth they could be saved only as individuals, in exactly the same way as the Gentiles. As a nation, they had been rejected as the chosen people. Here is the way the Bible describes that rejection:

- **Matthew 21:43** "The kingdom of God shall be taken from you."
- **Matthew 21:19** "And when he saw a fig tree in the way, he came to it, and found nothing thereon, but leaves only, and said unto it, Let no fruit grow on thee henceforward for ever. And presently the fig tree withered away." (The fig tree was a symbol of the Jewish nation.)
- **Matthew 23:38** "Behold, your house is left unto you desolate."
- **Galatians 3:28** "There is neither Jew nor Greek, there is neither bond nor free, there is neither male nor female: for ye are all one in Christ Jesus."
- **Galatians 3:29** "And if ye be Christ's, then are ye Abraham's seed, and heirs according to the promise."
- **Romans 10:12** "For there is no difference between the Jew and the Greek: for the same Lord over all is rich unto all that call upon him."
- **Romans 9:6–8** "For they are not all Israel, which are of Israel: Neither,

because they are the seed of Abraham, are they all children; but, In Isaac shall thy seed be called. That is, They which are … the children of the promise are counted for the seed." (The New Testament teaches the acceptance of spiritual Israel, and the rejection of physical Israel and the children of the flesh.)

- **Romans 2:28, 29** "For he is not a Jew, which is one outwardly; neither is that circumcision, which is outward in the flesh: But he is a Jew, which is one inwardly; and circumcision is that of the heart, in the spirit, and not in the letter."
- **Acts 13:46** "It was necessary that the word of God should first have been spoken to you: but seeing ye put it from you, and judge yourselves unworthy of everlasting life, lo, we turn to the Gentiles."

The rapturists get their seven years' tribulation by lifting that seventieth week of Daniel's prophecy completely out of its context and shoving it far into the future. They claim it will be fulfilled after Christ comes to snatch away the righteous secretly. Incredible? Absolutely! But they must grasp desperately for some text to support their seven years. They agree that the sixty-nine weeks of Daniel 9:25 refer to the period before Christ's first advent, but then they insert a 2,000-year gap before the seventieth week is fulfilled. They allot 69 weeks plus 2,000 years plus one week, or a total of 2,490 years. By this devious manipulation of God's Word, the rapturists believe they have extended the Jewish probation; and based upon this, they teach that all the fleshly Jews will be saved in a great second chance after the "secret rapture" takes place.

The tragedy of the rapture theory is that it takes these beautiful verses of Daniel 9:24–27 that predict the coming of Jesus, His baptism and crucifixion, and apply them to Antichrist. They do this by stating that it is Antichrist that causes the sacrifice and oblation to cease after three and one-half years. But Daniel states that it is Jesus who caused the sacrificial system of the Jews to cease when He died on the cross. A misinterpretation that confuses something Christ has done, and applies it to the devil instead, is certainly a tragic occurrence. And yet this is the only way one can arrive at a seven-year tribulation period. How sad!

FIVE
WHEN DOES THE ANTICHRIST APPEAR?

Now we are brought to focus on the most glaring inconsistency of the rapture theory, and that is that the Antichrist will not appear until after the saints are caught away—seven years before the end of the world. Paul settles the entire matter for us in the first few verses of 2 Thessalonians chapter 2. "Now we beseech you, brethren, by the coming of our Lord Jesus Christ, and by our gathering together unto him, That ye be not soon shaken in mind, or be troubled, neither by spirit, nor by word, nor by letter as from us, as that the day of Christ is at hand. Let no man deceive you by any means: for that day [of our gathering together unto Him] shall not come, except there come a falling away first, and that man of sin [Antichrist] be revealed, the son of perdition; Who opposeth and exalteth himself above all that is called God, or that is wor shipped; so that he as God sitteth in the temple of God, shewing himself that he is God" (vs. 1–4).

The words of Paul are so plain that it is difficult to comment on them. How can they be plainer? Christ's coming will not take place "except there come a falling away first, and that man of sin be revealed." Show these words to any child who has learned to read; show them to anyone not prejudiced by "private" interpretations, and he will say, "These verses say that the man of sin (Antichrist) is going to be revealed before Jesus comes."

Paul is not referring to some superman suddenly to appear 2,000 years after his epistles. He wrote, "For the mystery of iniquity doth already work" (v. 7). While Paul lived, he combated the emerging spirit of the Antichrist. By the sixth century A.D.,

Antichrist had matured. The crowning act in the great drama of deception, however, occurs just before the return of Christ: "And then shall that Wicked be revealed, whom the Lord shall consume with the spirit of his mouth, and shall destroy with the brightness of his coming" (v. 8). This clearly states that Antichrist will be destroyed when Christ comes. He does not arrive after the Second Advent.

And here's the crowning clarification in this whole thing. Revelation 20:4 assures us that some of those who are raised in the first resurrection will be those who refused to worship the beast and receive his mark! How completely this demolishes the futuristic school of prophetic interpretation is evident, for they claim that the emergence of the Antichrist and the imposition of his mark are to be looked for after the first resurrection and what they call the secret rapture. Recently a radio preacher expressed this belief: "I don't expect to be here when the beast is enforcing his mark upon the people. I expect to go up in the rapture and be in heaven during the great tribulation time." But these verses declare that some of those who come up in the "first resurrection," when Christ comes the second time, have already refused to worship the Antichrist or receive his mark! Thus, the Antichrist must have already been on the stage of action carrying on his oppressive work before the "first resurrection" and well before the second coming of Jesus.

Without attempting to establish the identity of Antichrist at this point, let us notice how this teaching—that the Antichrist will come in the future—originated. At the time of the Reformation, most of the reformers understood the prophecy of the Antichrist to refer to the great apostate system of Romanism that developed during the Middle Ages. Of course, Rome did not appreciate this interpretation. Please notice Rome's course of action to nullify this interpretation:

> "So great a hold did the conviction that the Papacy was the Antichrist gain upon the minds of men, that Rome at

last saw she must bestir herself, and try, by putting forth other systems of interpretation, to counteract the identification of the Papacy with the Antichrist.

"Accordingly, toward the close of the century of the Reformation, two of the most learned doctors set themselves to the task, each endeavoring by different means to accomplish the same end, namely, that of diverting men's minds from perceiving the fulfillment of the prophecies of the Antichrist in the papal system. The Jesuit Alcazar devoted himself to bring into prominence the preterist method of interpretation, … and thus endeavored to show that the prophecies of Antichrist were fulfilled before the popes ever ruled in Rome, and therefore could not apply to the Papacy.

"On the other hand, the Jesuit Ribera tried to set aside the application of these prophecies to the papal power by bringing out the futurist system, which asserts that these prophecies refer properly, not to the career of the Papacy, but to some future supernatural individual, who is yet to appear, and continue in power for three and a half years. Thus, as Alford says, the Jesuit Ribera, about A.D. 1580, may be regarded as the founder of the futurist system of modern times.

"It is a matter for deep regret that those who advocate the futurist system at the present day, Protestants as they are for the most part, are really playing into the hands of Rome, and helping to screen the Papacy from detection as the Antichrist."[1]

Thus, the whole theory of the secret rapture with its future Antichrist had its origin with the Jesuits in an attempt to take the blame off the Papacy.

The origin of the two-phase coming of Christ has an equally unsavory history. It was not until around the year 1830 that this view began to be taught. In the Scottish church pastored by Edward Irving, a Miss Margaret McDonald gave what was believed at the time to be an inspired utterance. She spoke of the visible, open, and glorious second coming of Christ. But as the utterance continued, she spoke of another coming of Christ—a secret and special coming in which those who were truly ready would be raptured.[2]

However, it was John Nelson Darby—a Brethren preacher and diligent writer of the time in England—who was largely responsible for introducing this new teaching on a large scale. The teaching spread to the United States in the 1850s and 1860s, where it was to receive its biggest boost when Cyrus Ingerson Scofield, a strong believer in Darby's teachings, incorporated it into the notes of his Scofield Reference Bible, which was published in 1909. Since that time, this view has been widely accepted often by people who are completely unaware that this was not the belief held by Christians over the centuries. Many fine Christians hold his view today who have never questioned its authority.

Oswald Smith, noted minister and author of Toronto, says in his booklet *Tribulation or Rapture—Which?* that he once held the two-stage teaching, but that when he began to search the Scriptures for himself, he discovered that there is not a single verse in the Bible to uphold this view. He confessed: "I had been taught that the Greek word 'parousia' always referred to the Rapture and that other words were used for the coming of Christ in glory … but I found that this is not true. … We might go through all the writers of the New Testament, and we would fail to discover any indication of the so-called 'two-stages' of our Lord's coming … That theory had to be invented by man. Search and see. There is no verse in the Bible that even mentions it."

SIX
The Second Chance

Finally, the secret rapturists claim that during the tribulation those not raptured will be given another chance to be saved.

Let it be categorically stated that nowhere does Scripture speak of a second chance, nor does the Bible anywhere speak of people being saved after Jesus comes. This is just another manmade doctrine that is indeed pleasing to the carnal heart of man. Actually, the Bible teaches the opposite. Notice these clear texts of Scripture:

- **2 Corinthians 6:2** "Behold, *now* is the *accepted time;* behold, *now is the day of salvation.*"
- **Revelation 22:11, 12** "He that is unjust, let him be unjust still: and he which is filthy, let him be filthy still: and he that is righteous, let him be righteous still: and he that is holy, let him be holy still. And, behold, I come quickly; and my reward is with me." (Evidently probation closes just prior to the Second Advent.)
- **Jeremiah 8:20** "The harvest (day of second coming) is past, the summer is ended, and we are *not* saved."

When Jesus comes the second time, He carries "in his hand a sharp sickle"

(Revelation 14:14). This is the reaping time after sixty centuries of the sowing of the seeds of sin. This is the harvest time, and "the harvest is the end of the world" (Matthew 13:39). "And he that sat on the cloud thrust in his sickle on the earth; and the earth was reaped" (Revelation 14:16). Truly did Jeremiah say, "The harvest is past … and we are not saved" (Jeremiah 8:20). There can be no saving after the reaping of earth's harvest at the coming of Christ.

When Jesus and His holy angels appear, then "before him shall be gathered all nations" (Matthew 25:32). There will only be two classes in that great company. The destiny of each has been set by what he did before the coming of Christ.

Let us stand firm on the Word of God alone and reject these manmade, man-pleasing ideas that form the bulk of the whole secret rapture theory. As we have noticed, the Bible clearly teaches that Jesus Christ will come the second time in glorious majesty to take His redeemed home with Him. It will be a personal, visible, and earthshaking event that everyone alive will know about. The righteous will be caught up to meet the Lord in the air (1 Thessalonians 4:17), whereas the wicked will be slain by the brightness of that coming (2 Thessalonians 2:8). Let us carefully study our Bibles that we will not be deceived concerning this most important and wonderful hope, the second coming of Jesus.

ENDNOTES

[1] Reverend Joseph Tanner, *Daniel and the Revelation,* pp. 16, 17. (See also L. E. Froom, *The Prophetic Faith of Our Fathers,* Vol 2, Review and Herald Publishing Association, 1950, pp. 484-510.)

[2] Dave MacPherson, *The Incredible Cover-up,* Logos International, 1975, Omega Publications, Medford, OR.